A Last Harvest

Philip Bourke Marston

Contents

To PHILIP BOURKE MARSTON 7
BIOGRAPHICAL SKETCH OF 7
PHILIP BOURKE MARSTON 7
LIGHT: AN EPTCEDE 19
TO PHILIP BOURKE MARSTON 19
LYRICS 21
LOVE'S LOST PLEASURE-HOUSE 21
LOVE'S LADY 22
ALAS! 24
MY LIFE PUTS FORTH TO SEA ALONE 25
FLOWN LOVE 26
A BAGATELLE 27
A CASTLE IN SPAIN 28
A SONG FOR TWILIGHT 28
THE RIVER 30
LOVE'S FLYING FEET 31
TO SLEEP 32
LOVERS 32
A REMEMBERED TUNE 33
AFTER LOVE'S PASSING 34
A QUESTION 35
HEART-BREAKS AND SONGS 36
LOOKING FORWARD, IN FEBRUARY 36
HER PITY 37
GO, SONGS OF MINE 38
AFTER SUMMER 39
AT LAST 40
LAST GARDEN SECRETS 41
ROSES AND THE NIGHTINGALE 41
FLOWER FAIRIES 43
THE LONELY ROSE 45
SUMMER CHANGES 46
A RUINED GARDEN 48
SONNETS 49
WHEN WITH THY LIFE THOU 49
DIDST ENCOMPASS MINE 49
THE BREADTH AND BEAUTY 50
OF THE SPACIOUS NIGHT 50
WHICH IS IT, LOVE? 50
HER ATMOSPHERE 51
LOVE ASLEEP 52
LOVE'S GHOST 52
APRIL 53
MY GRAVE 53
HER IN ALL THINGS 54

OF EARLY VIOLETS	54
BELLS OF LONDON	55
A COUNTRY'S GHOST	56
TO ALL SAD OF HEART	56
TO ALL IN HAVEN	57
FORECASTING	57
FRIENDSHIP AND LOVE	58
HERE IN THIS SUNSET SPLENDOUR DESOLATE	58
ALL ROUND ABOUT ME IS THE CITY'S NOISE	59
O YE WHO SAILED WITH ME	60
BELOVED OF HER	60
COULD IT BUT BE!	61
NOT ONLY ROOMS WHEREIN THY	61
LOVE HAS BEEN	61
WHAT WAILING WIND	62
I THOUGHT THAT I WAS HAPPY YESTERDAY	62
WHEN THOU ART FAR FROM ME	63
FOUR PARABLES	64
LOVE'S DESERTED PALACE	66
SPRING AND DESPAIR	67
LETHARGY	67
FROM LONDON STREETS	68
OUT OF SLEEP	68
RESIGNATION	69
TO-MORROW	69
SORROW'S GHOST	70
LONDON, FROM FAR	71
UNSHELTERED LOVE	71
WHEN IN THE DARKNESS I WAKE UP ALONE	72
A PRAYER TO SLEEP	72
I WALKED IN LOVE'S DESERTED ROOM	73
TO THE SPIRIT OF POETRY	73
OLD MEMORIES	74

A LAST HARVEST

BY

Philip Bourke Marston

To PHILIP BOURKE MARSTON

Sweet Poet, thou of whom these years that roll
Must one day yet the burdened birthright learn,
And by the darkness of thine eyes discern
How piercing was the sight within thy soul;—
Gifted, apart, thou goest to the great goal,
A cloud-bound, radiant spirit, strong to earn,
Light-reft, that prize for which fond myriads yearn
Vainly, light-blest,—the Seër's aureole.

And doth thine ear, divinely dowered to catch
All spheral sounds in thy song blent so well,
Still hearken for my voice's slumbering spell
With wistful love? oh! let the muse now snatch
My wreath for thy young brows, and bend to watch
Thy veiled transfiguring sense s miracle.

DANTE GABRIEL ROSSETTI.

BIOGRAPHICAL SKETCH OF PHILIP BOURKE MARSTON

'No ominous hour
Knocks at his door with tidings of mishap—
Far off is he above desire and fear.'

To write of Philip Bourke Marston is to speak of one at whom, through all his life, Fate seemed to mock; and yet I have sometimes felt, while reading his noble and beautiful verse, that many a man on whom Destiny has smiled would have considered such inspiration and such achievement as were the consolation of our blind poet cheaply purchased at cost of a life of commonplace happiness.

He was the son of Dr Westland Marston, himself both a poet and a dramatist, and a lineal descendant of John Marston, the play-wright of the sixteenth century. Philip was heir, it would have seemed, to an inheritance of good fortunes. His beautiful dark eyes opened on a world fair with love and hope. Philip James Bailey, the author of 'Festus,' was his godfather; and Dinah Maria Mulock (Mrs Craik) was his godmother. There were already two sisters—Eleanor and Ciceley—to welcome the baby brother born into their home on the 13th of August 1850. This newcomer was the idol of them all, and he began to be 'Philip, the King/ long before he could speak.

There were three years during which all the promises of Fate were fair. Then came that accident—a blow received while playing with some little companions—in consequence of which I should have said that he wholly lost his sight, save that he has so often insisted to me on the difference between seeing, as he did in his boyhood, (though dimly as through a mist), the fires that lit the sunset sky, the glow on the winter hearth, the trees waving with the wind's breath, the vague, phantom shapes of men and women walking like ghosts, and seeing, as was the case after he was twenty—nothing. Who can possibly measure the calamity of the loss of vision to a predestined poet?

Philip, of course, could never learn to read. His education came to him through the books that were read to him, and the talk of the clever and gifted people who were the guests of the household. There are few homes, indeed, to which such visitors came as to that London house near the Regent's Park, where Browning, and Thackeray, and Dickens, and Rossetti and Swinburne, and the best and brightest men and women of the time were frequent visitors.

Philip began to write—or rather to dictate to his mother, who was, as long as she lived, his loving and faithful amanuensis—when he had scarcely outgrown his pinafores ; and by the time he was fifteen he had written some really noteworthy verse that was afterwards included in his first volume. While he was beginning to arrange the poems for this first book, and when he was scarcely twenty, his mother died. He has talked to me sometimes of his passionate sorrow at her loss. He felt, then, as if the whole world 'had gone to pieces'; and for a while after that he could think of nothing but the love that had been, and was not.

It almost seemed like a miracle of mercy when he met Mary Nesbit; and her sweet young voice lured him back to a fresh interest in this world.

He loved her, as poets love—suddenly, romantically, and with an adoring and idealizing devotion that at once expressed itself in the fifty-seven sonnets which form the first division of his earliest book—'Song-Tide, and Other Poems.' The poems—the love—the lover—who knows what?—touched the girlish heart he sought to win, and moved it to response; and Mary Nesbit pledged herself to share the young poet's darkened life. In 1871—soon after this betrothal—'Song-Tide' was published and dedicated to the memory of Philip's mother. It was an immediate success. The best critics welcomed it with their approval—the Examiner even declared that, by virtue of this volume, the author should 'take an equal place alongside Swinburne, Morris, and Rossetti.' I have seen letters on letters of praise addressed to the young poet from such masters of song as Swinburne and Rossetti. In one of these, Rossetti wrote—'Only yesterday evening I was reading your "Garden Secrets" to William Bell Scott, who fully agreed with me that it is not too much to say of them that they are worthy of Shakespeare in his subtlest lyrical moods.'

Remembering the long sadness of Marston's life, I love to pause for a moment on just this height of being—to see him, at twenty-one, young, happy even in spite of his misfortunes, loving and beloved, welcomed by noble poets as among their own high kindred, full of eager hope, triumphant, as it seemed, against his fate!

But, alas, it was not for long-that he stood upon this summit of his fortunes.

In the November of 1871 Miss Nesbit died, of swift consumption; and then, indeed, the last gleam of light departed from the eyes that wept for her such bitter tears. Henceforth they beheld no more the pageantry of sunset, or the hearth-fire by which he and his sorrow sat, desolate, at night. But no! I must not speak of him as quite desolate; for Ciceley remained to him. His sister Eleanor was, by this time, married to Arthur O'Shaughnessy, himself a poet; but Ciceley, henceforth, until her own death, gave herself to be eyes and hands for this her stricken brother. It seemed almost as if his heart beat, his brain throbbed, in her body, so entirely was it the business and the pleasure of her life to do his will.

The house, near Regent's Park, where the family had lived so long, and which during the life-time of Mrs Marston had been the scene of so many brilliant symposia, was given up, and Philip and Ciceley henceforth lived together. They lived in London—which was Philip's birthplace and his lifelong home—but they traveled many times to France, and one golden year to Italy—that fair 'woman-country' which forever after haunted Philip's memory, as for many a longing year it had haunted his dreams. They worked together, too, and no sightless man can ever have been served more faithfully than was Philip while this sister of his mind as well as of his heart was spared to him.

It was perhaps a year after Miss Nesbit's death when her bereaved lover made the acquaintance of Oliver Madox Brown, the author of 'The Dwale Bluth,' 'The Black Swan,' and several other remarkable tales. He was the son of Ford Madox Brown, the well-known artist, and was himself a painter, as well as a novelist and a poet. His friendship was one of the supreme joys of Marston's life. The two met almost daily; and when anything kept them apart they wrote to each other. They planned conquests of art and of literature—they sympathized with each others ambitions—they were friends, in the uttermost sense of the word. At last Oliver became ill, from blood-poisoning; but though Philip was full of anxiety during his brief illness, the news of his death came with an awful shock of surprise and horror.

It was in 1874 that Oliver Madox Brown died; and before his sickness he had read some of the proofs and all the manuscript of 'All In All'—Marston's second volume of poems. 'Song-Tide,' as I said, had been inscribed to the memory of Philip's mother. 'All In All' was dedicated to his father, though all the poems it contained—with the exception of one to his sister Ciceley, with which the book concluded—were consecrated to the lost love whose young life had been pledged to his own.

A book so heart-breaking could scarcely win the ear of the pleasure-loving world as had the gayer music of 'Song-Tide,' written when life was at its full. Critics and poets, indeed, appreciated the sad dignity, the poignant pathos of 'All In All'— but the world at large craves sunshine and not shadow. No thoughtful reader, however, could ignore the nobility of many of these poems. I wish that the volume might be reprinted; but, indeed, I feel that there should be a complete edition of Philip Bourke Marston's Poems, including 'Song-Tide,' 'All In All,' 'Wind Voices,' and this 'Last Harvest,' gathered from his grave; for, surely, he was not 'the idle singer of an empty day,' but a poet, rather, who spoke to the deepest hearts of men, and whose words have a claim upon our hallowing memory.

His life was eventful only in its sorrows and in its friendships. He was but fourteen years old when he was first taken to see Swinburne, and at that time— wonderful as the achievement seems—he actually knew by heart the whole of the First Series of 'Poems and Ballads.' The friendship begun on that memorable day was a pride and a joy to Marston for all the rest of his life. Later on he came also to know intimately Dante Gabriel Rossetti, and to love him with adoring enthusiasm. One of Rossetti's latest sonnets was addressed to Marston. William Sharp, poet and novelist; Herbert E. Clarke, the poet; Theodore Watts, himself a poet, and the best critic of poetry who is writing at present; Coulson Kernahan, the brilliant young author of 'A Dead Man's Diary'; C. Churchill Osborne, the Hon. Roden Noel, A. Mary F. Robinson, Olive Schreiner, Iza Duffus Hardy, Mrs W. K. Clifford, E. Nesbit—these were a few, only, of the group of literary friends who cheered with their sympathy and appreciation the last sad years of

Marston's darkened life.

I, myself, first met him in 1876, on the first day of July—just six weeks before his twenty-sixth birthday. He was tall, slight, and in spite of his blindness, graceful. He seemed to me young-looking even for his twenty-six years. He had a noble and beautiful forehead. His brown eyes were perfect in shape, and even in colour, save for a dimness like a white mist that obscured the pupil, but which you perceived only when you were quite near to him. His hair and beard were dark brown, with warm glints of chestnut; and the colour came and went in his cheeks as in those of a sensitive girl. His face was singularly refined, but his lips were full and pleasure-loving, and suggested dumbly how cruel must be the limitations of blindness to a nature hungry for love and for beauty. I had been greatly interested, before seeing him, in his poems, and to meet him was a memorable delight.

He and the sister who was his inseparable companion soon became my close friends, and with them both this friendship lasted till the end.

In Ciceley's case the 'end' was not far distant. She came to see me, on the morning of July 28th, 1878, and complained, when she came in, that her head ached 'desperately.' I persuaded her to lie down; but, suddenly, she sprang to her feet, called my name, and fell back again, stricken with the 'foudroyant apoplexy' of which she died in the mid-afternoon of that same day. Philip and his father were travelling in France, just then; and as they were moving from place to place on their homeward way, we did not even know where to reach them with a telegram. They returned to London, therefore, in utter ignorance of their loss, to find the daughter and sister so beloved awaiting her burial.

I have always felt that this was the cruellest bereavement of Marston's life. When his mother, his betrothed, and his friend died, in sad and swift succession, there had always been Ciceley to comfort and console him. But when Ciceley went, there was no such survivor. His other sister was not only married, but was even then a chronic invalid. His father's health, also, was broken ; and devoted as he was to his son, he could not give him what Ciceley had given him of day-long companionship and constant service. It was after this loss of his sister that many of the new friends I have mentioned came into Philip's life; and to the list might be added various Americans, such as Mrs Laura Curtis Bullard, and three of our well-known poets, Edmund Clarence Stedman (who had spoken of Marston with earnest appreciation in his 'Victorian Poets,') Richard Watson Gilder, and the Southern poet, Paul Hamilton Hayne. From this time forth, a large proportion of Marston's work, both in prose and verse, was published in America, and won a wide audience among the best American readers.

As years went on he needed the comfort of friendship more than ever, for sorrow upon sorrow assailed him. His sister Eleanor died in the February of 1879; and his brother-in-law, Arthur O'Shaughnessy in the January of 1881. In the April of 1882 Dante Gabriel Rossetti—the enthusiasm of the blind poet's life—died in his turn, and in a sonnet to his memory Marston spoke of him as transcending all other men, and leading k the train of love.'

Marston's third volume of poems—'Wind Voices'—was published in 1883; by Eliot Stock, in London, and by Roberts Brothers, in America. It was certainly a distinct advance on the two preceding volumes in variety, and on the whole in strength; though no lyric in it surpassed 'The Wind and the Rose,' and perhaps no sonnet excelled two or three that might be selected from the previous volumes. That 'Wind Voices' was dedicated to myself, as a proof of its author's friendship, does not, I am sure, affect my judgment of it. I am convinced that it contains work which generations to come will value, as we value now the lovely legacies of song bequeathed to us by singers of old days. Unhappily it was not stereotyped, and the edition was swiftly exhausted. The best critics in England and in America reviewed it with such cordial praise that I like to remember the pleasure their words gave to him whose pleasures in those days were so few.

From that very time—the autumn of 1883—Marston's health began sensibly and visibly to decline. He was gay, still, when his friends were with him; for no man ever confronted the sorrows of his life more bravely, or made less claim on the compassion of his fellows. He wrote once:—

Of me ye may say many a bitter thing,
O Men, when I am gone, gone far away,
To that dim Land where shines no light of day.
Sharp was the bread for my soul's nourishing
Which Fate allowed, and bitter was the spring
Of which I drank and maddened, even as they
Who wild with thirst at sea will not delay,
But drink the brine and die of its sharp sting.
Not gentle was my war with Chance, and yet
I borrowed no man's sword—alone I drew,
And gave my slain fit burial out of view.
In secret places I and Sorrow met—
So when you count my sins, do not forget
To say I taxed not any one of you.

This sonnet was no idle boast. He had a delicate pride that always led him to prefer to confer favours rather than to receive them. Many of the sonnets in 'Wind Voices' were self-revealing to a degree that only those who knew him well could fully divine. In one—'A Question'—he asks himself whether the prevision of Death would have been ghastlier, had Life been full for him of joy; and he answers his own question thus:—

Harder seems this—to die and leave the sun,
And carry hence each unfulfilled desire.
I heard one cry, 'Come where the feast is spread,'
But when I came the festival was done:
Somewhile I shivered by the extinguished fire
And now retrace my steps uncomforted.

And, once again, he wrote:—

Still the old paths, and the old solitude,
And still the dark soul journeying on its way.

The journey was not to be long; yet the three years after the publication of 'Wind Voices' were so full of loneliness and of sadness that I cannot bear to think of them—though always and up to the very last, he could be blithe whenever there was anyone with whom to make merry; and small things sufficed to please and cheer him. He founded, during those years, a Club, to which he gave the name of 'The Vagabonds,' which used to meet for a monthly evening. This club survives him. It is 'The Vagabonds' still; and there have been numerous additions to its members. Marston's memory is its religion.

Philip clung, if possible, more closely than ever to his friends, because a low voice was forever whispering in his ear that his time for friendship was brief. He often said to me that his future would be short—but I could never quite believe it. How could I think that with so much affluence of life in the world it would be snatched from these young lips that thirsted for it so eagerly?

In the autumn of 1886, while in Brighton with his father, he was stricken with brain fever, and one of his delusions was that from his window (which looked upon a stone-paved yard), he could see great ships, with all their white sails set, sailing, all of them, to America, whither he had always hoped to go. 'They will stop for me, soon,' he used often to say. A ship stopped for him soon, indeed—too soon—but it was to bear him to a farther shore than the one of which he dreamed—over a sea unfathomed, to a port unknown.

I saw him in the autumn after this illness; and I was curiously and painfully struck with the vividness of his memory of long past things and his frequent forgetfulness of the engagements and the interests of the day. How often he said—'Why should I want to live? I really do not know why; but I shrink from that great mystery beyond. If I only knew!'

Through the winter of 1876-7 his letters—which came to me regularly, almost until the end—were far more brief than usual, and inexpressibly sad. He wrote that he was too weak to sit long at the type-writer, which, after Ciceley's death, he had learned to use for himself. How unutterably pathetic those mid-winter letters seem to me, when I recall them now! How they come back to me—vain cries out of the dark! 'If I only could sleep!' he wrote, again and again—and now sleep laps him round.

It was in the last of January that he experienced what then seemed only a slight shock of paralysis. On the first day of February he telegraphed his friend Herbert Clarke to come to him. Even then he could only speak with great difficulty, though he managed to say that he wanted to live, and hoped to get better. After that day he never spoke at all. His father wrote me how agonizing were his attempts to make himself understood; but this was at first. After a few days he gave up the struggle, and subsided into a gentle quietude, until, at last, 'he almost slept into Eternity.'

He died in the morning of February 14th, 1887. Had he lived till the 13th of the next August, he would have been thirty-seven years old. He was buried at Highgate Cemetery on the 18th of February. It was a grey and foggy day—as if the Earth, herself, were in mourning for him, her lover. Many friends wrote me how strangely beautiful was the dead poet's face; and one of them spoke of its extraordinary likeness to Severn's portrait of Keats. The coffin was heaped with wreaths of flowers, sent by friends near and far.

Even before his funeral—on the very day after his death—Swinburne had written so memorable an expression of his sorrow for his friend's loss that I must quote it here:—

The days of a man are threescore and ten.
The days of his life were half a man's, whom we
Lament, and would yet not bid him back to be
Partaker of all the woes and ways of men.
Life sent him enough of sorrow: not again

Would anguish of love, beholding him set free,
Bring back the beloved to suffer life, and see
No light but the fire of grief that scathed him then.

We know not at all: we hope and do not fear.
We shall not again behold him, late so near,
Who now from afar above, with eyes alight
And spirit enkindled, haply toward us here
Looks down, unforgetful yet, of days like night
And love that has yet his sightless face in sight.

Theodore Watts quoted, in the Athenœum, this tribute of Swinburne's, enshrining it in a prose memorial of his own, so beautiful that by no one who read it could it be forgotten. The illustrated papers published Marston's likeness, accompanied by sketches of his sad and too brief life. Praises were lavished on his work, as flowers had been upon his tomb; and he—he, who had so loved the sympathy and appreciation of his fellow men—was he deaf to it all, I wonder, down there where he was laid?

He had always so welcomed the spring—had sung its praises in so many a rhyme—and now the spring came on apace without him. As his friend Clarke wrote, in a 'Monody' too long for quotation here:—

The March wind buffets the blithe daffodils
Snowdrop and crocus the rough season dare;
A rumour of vague joy is on the hills,
Gladness of expectation holds the air;
And in the bright cold sunshine forth I fare.
And lo! a silent shadow at my side—
A sad and silent shadow everywhere,
Like to another self, goes stride for stride,
A wraith that with its desolate presence fills
The year's house, bare and wide.

I think that others, who were Philip's friends, recognise, sometimes, this silent shadow at our side. It almost seems as if he were but veiled from us by some unfriendly cloud, and that he must know, still, all that concerns his fame, yes—even these poor words I write.

He had published a good many stories—he used to call them his pot-boilers; and after his death a volume of them was collected by his friend, William Sharp, and published under the title of 'For a Song's Sake, and Other Stories.' Some of these tales are so original and so clever as to persuade us that a veritable and note-worthy success in fiction might have been easily possible to him had the conditions of his life been more favourable. Such stories as, for instance, 'Miss Stotford's Specialty,' and 'Bryanstone and Wife,' justify the praise that has been bestowed on Marston's prose by so note-worthy a critic as Edmund Clarence Stedman. It is always the prose of a poet. Looking at his published and his unpublished work—a manuscript novel (his first attempt at fiction); his stories short and long, his brief essays, his critical reviews (chiefly published in the Athenœum), and his many poems, I am filled with amazement at the numerous and varied achievements of this young and blind man who fought his battle of life against such terrible odds.

Two other books, beside the volume of his stories, have been compiled from Marston's works since his death. For the first of these two—'Garden Secrets'—I am myself responsible. It had long been a favourite project of Marston's to publish, sometime, as he used to say, 'a little book,' with only the Garden poems in it—the secrets the flowers had whispered to him. With this his long-cherished wish in mind, I arranged the volume, in the spring after his death, and it was published—in 1887—by Roberts Brothers, Boston. Later on Mr Sharp compiled for publication in the 'Canterbury Poets' series, a book of selections from Marston's three previously printed volumes of poems. It represents his work fairly enough, perhaps, for the general reader; but does not, in my opinion, detract from the desirableness of a complete edition of all the verse which is this poet's legacy to the world. The present volume—'A Last Harvest' is composed of poems not included in the previous books. They were the fruit of the three sad, last years of Marston's life. They are not wholly sad, however—though, in those last years, sadness rested upon him like a pall. Even those who are happy may care, sometimes, to listen to the passion and the pathos of a sorrow they themselves have never known; and to the heavy of heart there is a gleam of comfort in the knowledge that other hearts have ached with a kindred pain—that they are not pioneers in the desolate path of grief. Swinburne was not at fault, when he wrote, in that February darkened by Marston's death—

'Thy song may soothe full many a soul hereafter.'

But indeed, I must quote the whole of the noble poem, which though written almost before the sod had been heaped upon Philip's grave, appeared, for the first time, in the Fortnightly Review for January, 1891.

LIGHT: AN EPTCEDE

TO PHILIP BOURKE MARSTON

Love will not weep because the seal is broken
That sealed upon a life beloved and brief
Darkness, and let but song break through for token
How deep, too far for even thy song's relief,
Slept in thy soul the secret springs of grief.
Thy song may soothe full many a soul hereafter,
As tears, if tears will come, dissolve despair;
As here but late, with smile more bright than laughter,
Thy sweet, strange, yearning eyes would seem to bear
Witness that joy might cleave the clouds of care.

Ten days agone, and love was one with pity
When love gave thought wings towards the glimmering goal

Where, as a shrine lit in some darkling city,
Shone soft the shrouded image of thy soul;
And now thou art healed of life, art healed and whole.

Yea, two days since, all we that loved thee pitied;
And now with wondering love, with shame of face,
We think how foolish now, how far unfitted
Should be from us, toward thee who hast run thy race,
Pity—toward thee, who hast won the pitiless place:

The painless world of death, yet unbeholden
Of eyes that dream what light now lightens thine
And will not weep. Thought yearning toward those olden,
Dear hours that sorrow sees, and sees not shine,
Bows tearless down before a flameless shrine.

A flameless altar here of love and sorrow
Quenched and consumed together. These were one,
One thing for thee, as night was one with morrow,
And utter darkness with the sovereign sun;
And now thou seest life, sorrow and darkness done.

And yet love yearns again to win thee hither;
Blind love, and loveless, and unworthy thee;
Here where I watch the hours of darkness wither,
Here where mine eyes were glad and sad to see
Thine that could see not mine, though turned on me.

But now, if aught beyond sweet sleep lie hidden,
And sleep be sealed not fast on dead men's sight
Forever, thine hath grace for ours forbidden,
And sees as compassed round with change and night;
Yet light like thine is ours if love be light.

If the dead know anything, then surely this poem, written by a poet who had been the very earliest object of Marston's boyish enthusiasm, must have thrilled his silent heart to pride and joy. And if the dead know anything, warm indeed must have been the welcome which Dr Westland Marston received—on the fifth of January, 1890—from the son who had preceded him to the Stranger's Country by a month less than three years. Few fathers, surely, ever mourned for a son as that father mourned. His days and nights were passed in seeking for some sign that the dead had not forgotten him. And sometimes, in answer to his yearning, he seemed to hear a voice, to which all other ears were deaf, that whispered to him, from out the unknown world, of love that was immortal.

Father, mother, sisters and brother—surely they are all together, now, somewhere. For them is peace after tumult—rest after weariness—plenty after famine. to us the memory of a joy and a sorrow—the echo of a song.

Louise Chandler Moulton.

July 1891.

LYRICS

LOVE'S LOST PLEASURE-HOUSE

LOVE built for himself a Pleasure-House—
A Pleasure-House fair to see—
The roof was gold, and the walls thereof
Were delicate ivory.

Violet crystal the windows were,
All gleaming and fair to see—
Pillars of rose-stained marble up-bore

That house where men longed to be.

Violet, golden, and white and rose,
That Pleasure-House fair to see
Did show to all, and they gave Love thanks
For work of such mastery.

Love turned away from his Pleasure-House,
And stood by the salt deep sea—
He looked therein, and he flung therein
Of his treasure the only key.

Now never a man till time be done
That Pleasure-House fair to see
Shall fill with music and merriment,
Or praise it on bended knee.

LOVE'S LADY

TO-DAY, as when we sat together close,
A great wind wakes and thunders as it blows—
We were together then beside the sea,
And now instead the sea between us flows.

O day that found us on that wind-swept coast,
And did such brave things for the future boast—
Though in thy voice a note of warning was—
This day, so like thee, seems thy very ghost!

O parted, precious, memorable days,
When sudden summer kindled all my ways,
When Love reached out his blessing hand to me,
And turned on mine the glory of his face!

And thou, my Love, in whose deep soul my soul
Lay for a little season and grew whole—
Thou who wert heat and light and sun and shade—
Thou who didst lead me to Life's fairest goal—

Whose sweetest lips Love, kissing, made to sing—
Ah, at what bright unfathomable spring
Was thy life nurtured, in the far-off land
Through which the unborn host go wandering?

In stately body God thy soul did clothe—
Thy perfect soul—that so thou mightst have both
To take away the hearts of men, withal;
And tenderness to strength He did betroth;

And in thy beautiful and luminous eyes
The wayward changefulness of April skies
He set for sovereign charm; and made thy voice
A sweet and a perpetual surprise.

Alas, what song of mine can demonstrate
The love that came between me and my fate—
That would have saved me from despair and Doom
Had Destiny but been compassionate?

As high as Heaven it was, deep as the sea,
And mystical and pure as lilies be,
And glowing with the glory of the June,
When birds and flowers and light make revelry.

Steadfast it was, as stars whereby men steer—
Tender as twilight, when the moon is near

And all the gentle air is warm with hope,
And we the Summer's hastening feet can hear.

How can my single, singing strength suffice
To worship thee, my Love, my Paradise?
My song falls weak before thee, and abashed,
Nor ever to thy spirit's height may rise;

Yet even by its failure men shall see
How more than all loves was my love of thee—
Thou, who didst overflow my life with Heaven
Making that life Love's miracle to be!

And, though my little note of music pass
As barren breath one breathes upon a glass,
And I be numbered with the numberless throng
Of whom men say not, even, 'This man was,'

O yet, from thee, in whom all beauty blent,
My Rose of women, from thy heart there went—
From thy deep, splendid, perfect, passionate heart—
A love to be, in death, my monument!

ALAS!

ALAS for all high hopes and all desires!
Like leaves in yellow autumn-time they fall—
Alas for prayers and psalms and love's pure fires—
One silence and one darkness ends them all!

Alas for all the world—sad fleeting race!
Alas, my Love, for you and me Alas!
Grim Death will clasp us in his close embrace

We, too, like all the rest from earth must pass.

Alas to think we must forget some hours
Whereof the memory like Love's planet glows—
Forget them as the year her withered flowers—
Forget them as the June forgets the rose!

Our keenest rapture, our most deep despair,
Our hopes, our dreads, our laughter, and our tears
Shall be no more at all upon the air—
No more at all, through all the endless years.

We shall be mute beneath the grass and dew
In that dark Kingdom where Death reigns in state—
And you will be as I, and I as you—
One silence shed upon us, and one fate.

MY LIFE PUTS FORTH TO SEA ALONE

My life puts forth to sea alone;
The skies are dark above;
All round I hear grey waters moan—
Alas for vanished love!

'O lonely life that presseth on
Across these wastes of years—
Where are the guiding pilots gone—
Whose is the hand that steers?'
The pilots they are left behind
Upon yon golden strand;
We drift before the driving wind;
We cannot miss the land—
That land to which we hurry on

Across the angry years;
Hope being dead, and sweet Love gone,
There is no hand that steers.

FLOWN LOVE

So far Love has flown we cannot find him;
All joy is past:
We may not follow, regain and bind him,
He flies so fast.

'And where has Love flown, if flown he be?
Can you not say?
Across what mountains, and over what sea?
Which way? which way?'

O'er viewless mountains and seas you know not,
To lands unknown,
Where winds are still, and where waters flow not:
There has Love flown.

'And when did Love leave you alone, alone?
Heart, say this thing.'
In the autumn-time, when the wet winds moan,
And dead leaves cling;

When the night was wildest, the sky most black,
At dead of night,
Right into the wind, on his trackless track,
Love took his flight.

'Oh wait till the summer the earth redeems
From winter's spell:

Then Love shall return and fulfil your dreams,
And all be well.'

Nay, Love shall not come with the lengthening light—
O Love flown far,
Right into the land, deep into the night
That knows no star.

A BAGATELLE

Not all the roses God hath made
Can love the sun aright:
The white rose is too chastely staid
To praise his warmth and light—
But great red roses, they can love
With their deep hearts their king above.

Nor nightingales by night that sing
Can love alike the moon;
Nor all the flowers that come with Spring
Can praise aright her boon—
One nightingale most feels Night's power,
And Spring is dearest to one flower.

Not all the gulls that skim the sea
Delight alike in storm;
And never man, Sweetheart, to thee
Gave love so true and warm
As mine, that Heaven ordained on high
To worship thee until I die.

A CASTLE IN SPAIN

To that country fair and far,
Where so many castles are,
Go, Song, on thy way!
Grand my castle once to see—
Home of light and revelry—
What is it to-day?

Round its turrets, fallen, lonely,
Dreams and songs now wander only,
Dreams and saddest song:
Dreary looks it in the noonlight—
Ghosts possess it in the moonlight,
When the night is long.

O my castle, fallen, lowly,
Fittest home for melancholy,
Sad, deserted place;
In your cold and crumbling halls,
Never now her footstep falls—
Never smiles her face!

A SONG FOR TWILIGHT

Now the winds a-wailing go
Through the sere forsaken trees:
Now the day is waxing low,
And above the troubled seas
Faint stars glimmer, and the breeze

Hovers, sad with memories.

Now the time to part has come,
What is left for us to say?
Shall we wander sad and dumb
Down this garden's leaf-strewn way,
Or by tossing waves and grey
Hand in hand together stray?

In this garden shall we stand,
In the day's departing light,—
Here, where first I touched your hand
On that unforgotten night
When you stood,' mid roses bright,
Dream, embodied to the sight?

Where we met, Love, shall we part?
In this garden shall we twain,
Mouth to mouth, as heart to heart,
Loving turn, and kiss again—
In this garden shall we drain
Love's last bitter-sweet, and pain?

Nay, Love, let us leave this place;
Let us go, Dear, to the beach
Where in happy summer days,
Sleeping Love awoke to speech;
And his voice though low, could reach
To the deepest heart of each.

There the sea-winds drifting sweet
From some strange land far away,
And the blown waves as they meet

One another in the bay—
These together haply may
Hint some word for us to say.

Let us kiss, then, Dear, and go
Down together to the sea;
We will kiss, Dear, meeting so,
In the days that are to be
If my heart should then be free,
If you should remember me!

THE RIVER

Suggested by the Fifteenth Prelude of Chopin

THE river flows forever—
The moon upon it shines—
One walks beside the river
With heart that longs and pines

A breeze moves on the river,
The moon shakes in its flow—
He grieves and grieves forever,
For days of long ago.

The softly lapsing river,
It whispers in its flow
Of dear days gone forever,
Those days of long ago.

He listens to the river,
A spirit seems to say—
'Forever, Love, forever,

Some day, some blessed day!'

Between the moon and river
The spirit seems to glide—
He cries—'To-night, forever,
I'll clasp thee, O my bride!'

And the happy pilgrim river,
As it journeys toward the sea,
Sings, 'Ever and forever,
Together they shall be!'

LOVE'S FLYING FEET

O FOLLOW Love's flying feet—
They're fleet as the Wind's and fleeter—
O honey indeed is sweet,
But the kisses of Love are sweeter.

O hark to the voice of Love!
The song of the lark as he rises,
Or the cry of the bird in a grove
That the light of a brooklet surprises

Is not so glad as Love's voice—
That voice that of all things is gladdest—
For it whispers of delicate joys,
And of raptures dearest and maddest.

O look in Love's eyes that shine,
Alight with the whole world's splendour:
They are stars, intense and divine,
In a passionate heaven and tender.

O worship Love while you may—
For never a love-dream may follow,
Where, hid from the light of the day,
Man sleeps in his small earth-hollow.

TO SLEEP

AH stay, dear Sleep, a little longer yet,
Though Day be come to chase thee—
And let me in thy sheltering arms forget—
Dear Sleep, once more embrace me!

The time will come when thou and I must part,
But now, Belovfed, linger,
And soothe once more the sad and weary heart
Of me, thy lover and singer!

Dear Comforter, who reignest undefiled—
Within thy kingdom holy
The weary man is even as a child—
The lofty as the lowly—

Ah, when our nuptial day shall dawn on high—
With nuptial love-fires lighted—
Then I for ever in thine arms shall lie,
By no fresh grief affrighted.

LOVERS

O WHAT does the Night-wind say to the rose?
Alas, there is never a heart that knows—

O what does the nightingale there in the brake
Sing to his love, as he sings for her sake?

Be glad there is never an ear to discover—
O sweet wind lover, O sweet bird lover!
Your secret is safe, as mine own shall be
When the lips that I love have breathed it to me

A REMEMBERED TUNE

My hand strayed o'er the piano keys,
And it chanced on a song that you sang, my dear,
When we roamed through the country stillnesses,
Or stood by the sea, when the moon was clear,
In that other year.

I forget the words you were wont to sing,
But the tune was a sweet and a tender one,
And sad as the thought of youth and Spring
To him who dreams, in the fading sun,
That the sweet time's done.

As I play, old hopes and old sorrows move,
Till it almost seems that your voice I hear,
And my spirit goes forth, to-day, to rove
Down the inland way where the sea was near,
In that other year.

As a bird that finds its nest
When the winds are overstrong,
With quivering wings and panting breast,
Even so to-day this song
Which your dear lips used to sing,

From the days long left behind
Enters now, and folds its wing
In the still, remembering mind.

AFTER LOVE'S PASSING

THE awful stillness in two human souls
Whence Love has passed away,
The dreary night no moon of joy controls
The undelightful day—

The cruel coldness where was once Love's heat,
The darkness where was light,
The burning tearless eyes, the weary feet
That journey day and night—

The long dark way that has no end but one—
That goal no man may miss—
The winds that wail about the sunken sun
For life's departed bliss—

The fearful loneliness that comes between
Those souls erst one, now twain—
The passionate memory of what has been;
The unavailing pain—

The springs that come, but bring no hope of change;
The cheerless, summer hours;
With songs of birds grown old, and harsh, and strange,
And scentless, bloomless flowers—

The fruitless autumn, with no garnered corn,
The dreary, winter weather—

The two who walk apart, alone, forlorn,
Who once kept step together—

The bitter sense of failure and regret,
The life without an aim,
The unavailing struggle to forget
The weakness, owned with shame—

These things make sad the night and sad the day,
And hard are they to bear—
Yet let those souls whence Love has passed away
Though sad, keep pure and fair:

Ah, let them say, 'Great Love once tarried here
Making his home divine—
Though he has passed, yet let us still hold dear
The temple and the shrine.'

A QUESTION

ONCE at this window, touched by climbing boughs
Whose plenteous leaves were quivering listlessly
With some least breath of wind, through the still house,
Borne from the dim, remote old library,
I heard the organ's music, slow, profound,
A moon-thrilled, travelling twilight of sweet sound,
Sad as the last breath of the leaves that lie
Thick, dead, and autumn-coloured on the ground.

To-day a child with eager hands will try
To gain the secret of the organ's soul,
And waking it to simple melody
Smile with fond pride to think he has the whole:—

Shall I, who know of old the stops and keys,
The pain and longing, the regret and peace
That stronger fingers waken and control,
Hurt his young heart by mocking him with these?

HEART-BREAKS AND SONGS

HEART-BREAKS and songs—
Fate, leave us these—
Since no man prolongs
Love's joy and peace.

Summer was fair,
Though it was fleet—
Cold now the air—
No breath is sweet.

Faint is the sun—
Roses are dead—
Lingers not one,
Dear, for your head.

Heart-breaks and songs—
Fate leave us these—
Since no man prolongs
Love's joy and peace.

LOOKING FORWARD, IN FEBRUARY

I LOOK across the brief, remaining space

Of chill and wintry days,
Till March to sprinkle violets shall begin,
And snow-drops white and thin.

I look through April, quick with scent and song,
To where the shining throng
Of laughing, garlanded May days come on,
With large light of the sun.

I look to June—fair flower of all the year—
O month of months appear!
O ardours of the summer time come close,
With nightingale and rose!

Make haste to come, O time of all delight—
Bright day, and tender night—
For then shall I within a Heaven dwell
Whose name Love may not tell.

HER PITY

THIS is the room to which she came that day—
Came when the dusk was falling cold and grey—
Came with soft step, in delicate array,

And sat beside me in the firelight there:
And like a rose of perfume rich and rare
Thrilled with her sweetness the environing air.

We heard the grind of traffic in the street—
The clamorous calls—the beat of passing feet—
The wail of bells that in the twilight meet.

Then I knelt down, and dared to touch her hand—
Those slender fingers, and the shining band
Of happy gold wherewith her wrist was spanned.

Her radiant beauty made my heart rejoice;
And then she spoke, and her low pitying voice
Was like the soft, pathetic, tender noise

Of winds that come before a summer rain:
Once leaped the blood in every clamorous vein—
Once leaped my heart, then dumb, stood still again.

GO, SONGS OF MINE

Go, songs of mine to bring her on her way
With whisperings of love:
'Tis bleak March now, but then it shall be May,
With gentle skies above
And gentle seas below, what time she hears
Your little music chiming in her ears.

Cold, cold this day, and white the air with snow,
And dark this place wherefrom
My hastening music ever loves to go
To find its natural home—
Its home with her to whom all charms belong;
Who is both Queen of Love and Queen of Song.

Shall glad spring come? Shall May come with warm hours
And laughter of clear light,
And blossoming trees, and festivals of flowers,
And nightingales by night, That pour their shuddering sweetness on the air—
The music of an exquisite despair?

And shall she come, who is my Spring of springs—
Herself than May more fair?
Sweet is the song the Night's sad songster sings,
But her tones are more rare—
Ah, shall she come, who is Spring and Summer in one—
To my sad life its star, its moon, its sun?

AFTER SUMMER

WE'LL not weep for summer over—
No, not we;
Strew above his head the clover—
Let him be!

Other eyes may weep his dying,
Shed their tears
There upon him, where he's lying
With his peers.

Unto some of them he proffered
Gifts most sweet—
For our hearts a grave he offered:
Was this meet?

All our fond hopes, praying, perished
In his wrath—
All the lovely dreams we cherished
Strewed his path.

Shall we in our tombs, I wonder,
Far apart,
Sundered wide as seas can sunder

Heart from heart,

Dream at all of all the sorrows
That were ours—
Bitter nights, more bitter morrows—
Poison-flowers

Summer gathered, as in madness,
Saying, 'See,
These are yours, in place of gladness—
Gifts from me?'

Nay, the rest that will be ours,
Is supreme—
And below the poppy flowers
Steals no dream.

AT LAST

REST here, at last,
The long way overpast—
Rest here, at home—
Thy race is run,
Thy dreary journey done, Thy last peak clomb.

'Twixt birth and death,
What days of bitter breath
Were thine, alas!
Thy soul had sight
To see, by day, by night,
Strange phantoms pass.

Thy restless heart

In few glad things had part,
But dwelt alone,
And night and day,
In the old way Made the old moan.

But here is rest
For aching brain and breast,
Deep rest, complete,
And nevermore,
Heart-weary and foot-sore,
Shall stray thy feet—
Thy feet that went
With such long discontent
Their wonted beat,
About thy room,
With its deep-seated gloom,
Or through the street.

Death gives them ease—
Death gives thy spirit peace—
Death lulls thee, quite—
One thing alone
Death leaves thee of thine own—
Thy starless night.

LAST GARDEN SECRETS

ROSES AND THE NIGHTINGALE

IN my garden it is night-time,
But a still time and a bright time,
For the moon rains down her splendour,

And my garden feels the wonder
Of the spell which it lies under
In that light so soft and tender.

While the moon her watch is keeping
All the blossoms here are sleeping,
And the roses sigh for dreaming
Of the bees that love to love them
When the warm sun shines above them
And the butterflies pass gleaming.

Could one follow roses' fancies,
When the night the garden trances,
Oh, what fair things we should chance on!
For to lilies and to roses,
As to us, soft sleep discloses
What the waking may not glance on.

But hark! now across the moonlight,
Through the warmness of the June night,
From the tall trees' listening branches
Comes the sound, sustained and holy,
Of the passionate melancholy,
Of a wound which singing staunches.

Oh, the ecstasy of sorrow
Which the music seems to borrow
From the thought of some past lover
Who loved vainly all his lifetime,
Till death ended peace and strife-time,
And the darkness clothed him over!

Oh, the passionate, sweet singing,

Aching, gushing, throbbing; ringing,
Dying in divine, soft closes,
Recommencing, waxing stronger,
Sweet notes, ever sweeter, longer,
Till the singing wakes the roses!

Quoth the roses to the singer:
'Oh, thou dearest music-bringer,
Now our sleep so sweetly endeth,
Tell us why thy song so sad seems,
When the air is full of glad dreams,
And the bright moon o'er us bendeth.'
Sang the singer to the roses:
'Love for you my song discloses—
Hence the note of grief I borrow.'
Quoth the roses, 'Love means pleasure.'
Quoth the singer, 'Love's best measure
Is its pure attendant sorrow.'

FLOWER FAIRIES

FLOWER fairies—have you found them,
When the summer's dusk is falling,
With the glow-worms watching round them,
Have you heard them softly calling?

Silent stand they through the noonlight,
In their flower shapes, fair and quiet,
But they hie them forth by moonlight,
Ready then to sing and riot.

I have heard them—I have seen them,
Light from their bright petals raying—

And the trees bent down to screen them,
Great, wise trees, too old for playing.

Hundreds of them, all together—
Flashing flocks of flying fairies—
Crowding through the summer weather,
Seeking where the coolest air is.

And they tell the trees that know them,
As upon their boughs they hover,
Of the things that chance below them,—
How the rose has a new lover—

And the gay Rose laughs, protesting,
'Neighbour Lily is as fickle':—
Then they search where birds are nesting,
And their feathers softly tickle.

Then away they all dance, sweeping,
Having drunk their fill of gladness;
But the trees, their night-watch keeping,
Thrill with tender pitying sadness;

For they know of bleak December,
When each bough left cold and bare is—
When they only shall remember
The bright visits of the fairies—

When the roses and the lilies
Shall be gone, to come back never
From the land where all so still is
That they sleep and sleep for ever.

THE LONELY ROSE

'To a heaven far away
Went the Red Rose when she died:'
So I heard the White Rose say,
As she swayed from side to side
In the chill October blast!
In the garden leaves fall fast—
This of roses is the last.

Said the White Rose, 'O my Red Rose,
O my Rose so fair to see,
When like thee I am a dead rose
Shall I in thy heaven be?'
O the drear October blast!
In the garden leaves fall fast—
This of roses is the last

'From that heavenly place, last night,
To me in a dream she came—
Stood there in the pale moonlight,
And she seemed, my Rose, the same.'
O the chill October blast!
In the garden leaves fall fast—
This of roses is the last.

'Only it maybe, perchance,
That her leaves were redder grown,
And they seemed to thrill and dance
As by gentle breezes blown.'
O the drear October blast!
In the garden leaves fall fast—

This of roses is the last

'And she told me, sweetly singing,
Of that heavenly place afar
Where the air with song is ringing,
Where the souls of all flowers are.'

O the chill October blast!
In the garden leaves fall fast—
This of roses is the last.

'And she bade me not to fail her,
Not to lose my heart with fear
When I saw the skies turn paler
With the sickness of the year—

I should be beyond the blast
And the leaves now falling fast
In that heavenly place at last.'

SUMMER CHANGES

SANG the Lily and sang the Rose,
Out of the heart of my garden close:—
'O joy, O joy of the summer tide!'
Sang the Wind, as it moved above them:—
'Roses were made for the wind to love them,
Dear little buds, in the leaves that hide!'

Sang the trees, as they rustled together:—
'O the joy of the summer weather!
Roses and lilies, how do you fare?'
Sang the Red Rose, and sang the White:—

'Glad we are of the Sun's large light,
And the songs of birds that dart through the air.'

Lily, and Rose, and tall green Tree,
Swaying boughs where the bright birds be,
Thrilled by music, and trembling with wings,
How glad they were on that summer day!
Little they recked of skies cold and grey,
Or the dreary dirge that a Storm-wind sings.

Golden butterflies gleam in the sun,
Laugh at the flowers and kiss each one;
And great bees come, with their sleepy tune,
To sip their honey, and circle round;
And the flowers are lulled by that drowsy sound,
And fall asleep in the heart of the noon.

A small white cloud in a sky of blue:
Roses and Lilies, what will they do?
For a wind springs up and sings in the trees:
Down comes the rain: the garden's awake:
Roses and Lilies begin to quake,
That were rocked to sleep by the gentle breeze.

Ah Roses and Lilies! Each delicate petal
The wind and the rain together unsettle—
This side and that side the tall trees sway:
But the wind goes by, and the rain stops soon,
And the shadow lifts from the face of the noon,
And the flowers are glad in the sun's warm ray.

Sing, my Lilies, and sing, my Roses,
With never a dream that the summer closes;

But the trees are old, and I fancy they tell,
Each unto each, how the summer flies:
They remember the last year's wintry skies;
But that Summer returns, the trees know well.

A RUINED GARDEN

ALL my roses are dead in my Garden—
What shall I do?
Winds in the night, without pity or pardon,
Came there and slew.

All my song-birds are dead in their bushes—
Woe for such things!
Robins and linnets and blackbirds and thrushes
Dead, with stiff wings.

Oh, my Garden! rifled and flowerless,
Waste now and drear:
Oh, my Garden! barren and bowerless,
Through all the year.

Oh, my dead birds! each in his nest there,
So cold and stark;
What was the horrible death that pressed there
When skies were dark?

What shall I do for my roses' sweetness,
The summer round—
For all my Garden's divine completeness
Of scent and sound?

I will leave my Garden for winds to harry;

Where once was peace,
Let the bramble-vine and the wild brier marry,
And greatly increase.

But I will go to a land men know not—
A far, still land,
Where no birds come, and where roses blow not
And no trees stand—

Where no fruit grows, where no spring makes riot,
But, row on row,
Heavy, and red, and pregnant with quiet
The poppies blow.

And there shall I be made whole of sorrow,
Have no more care—
No bitter thought of the coming morrow,
Or days that were.

SONNETS

WHEN WITH THY LIFE THOU DIDST ENCOMPASS MINE

WHEN with thy life thou didst encompass mine,
And I beheld, as from an infinite height,
Thy love stretch pure and beautiful as light,
Through extreme joy I hardly could divine
Whether my love of thee it was, or thine
Which so my heart astonished with its might.
But now, at length, familiar to the sight

So I can bear to look where planets shine,
Ever more deep the wonder grows to be
That thou shouldst love me, while my love of thee
Does of my very nature seem a part—
So, often now, as from a dream, I start,
To think that thou—even thou—thou lovest me,
I being what I am; thou what thou art.

THE BREADTH AND BEAUTY OF THE SPACIOUS NIGHT

THE breadth and beauty of the spacious night
Brimmed with white moonlight, swept by windsthat blew
The flying sea-spray up to where we two
Sat all alone, made one in Love's delight—
The sanctity of sunsets palely bright,
Autumnal woods, seen' neath meek skies of blue,
Old cities that God's silent peace stole through—
These of our love were very sound and sight:

The strain of labour; the bewildering din
Of thundering wheels; the bells' discordant chime;
The sacredness of art, the spell of rhyme—
These, too, with our dear love were woven in,
That so, when parted, all things might recall
The sacred love that had its part in all.

WHICH IS IT, LOVE?

WHICH is it, Love, enthralls me more to-night,
Quickening the pulses' throb and the heart's beat—
The memory of joy so subtly sweet

It wakes at thought, as when one plays aright
Some air to which Love's tones were wont to plight
The dearest singing words, till with the heat
Of passionate remembrance he can cheat
The heart that longs so even in Death's despite—

Or is it expectation of fresh bliss—
That bliss which Memory can so poorly feign,—
Deep joy of the anticipated kiss
Quickening the jubilant blood in every vein?
Thought of past joy, or joy to come again;
Confused by Love, I know not which it is.

HER ATMOSPHERE

WHAT of her soul's immaculate atmosphere,
Which all who know her breathe, which he knows best
Whose heart her love transfigured, saved and blest?
Buoyant as is the spring of the young year,
Tender as twilight when the moon is near,
Ardent as noon, and deep as midnights rest,
Pure as the air on heights no foot has prest,
That unto Heaven aspire, to Heaven are dear:—

A rareness, and a fragrance, and a sweetness,
A wonder and a glory without bound,
Such is her atmosphere's divine completeness,
A moving Paradise of sight and sound.
Blest She, in whom dear Heaven, dear Earth combine—
How shall they reach her, these weak words of mine?

LOVE ASLEEP

I FOUND Love sleeping in a place of shade,
And as in some sweet dream the sweet lips smiled;
Yea, seemed he as a lovely, sleeping child.
Soft kisses on his full, red lips I laid,
And with red roses did his tresses braid—
Then pure, white lilies on his breast I piled,
And fettered him with woodbine sweet and wild,
And fragrant armlets for his arms I made.

But while I, leaning, yearned across his breast,
Upright he sprang, and from swift hand, alert,
Sent forth a shaft that lodged within my heart.
Ah, had I never played with Love at rest,
He had not wakened, had not cast his dart,
And I had lived who die now of this hurt.

LOVE'S GHOST

Is it the ghost of dead and buried Love
Which haunts the House of Life, and comes by night
With weary sighs, and in its eyes the light
Of joys long set? I hear its footsteps move
Through darkened rooms where only ghosts now rove—
The rooms Love's shining eyes of old made bright;
It whispers low—it trembles into sight—
A bodiless presence hearts alone may prove.

I say, 'Sad visitant of this dark house,
Why wanderest thou through these deserted rooms,

A dreadful glimmering light about thy brows?
Thy silent home should be among the tombs.'
And the Ghost answers, while I thrill with fear,
In all the world I have no home but here.'

APRIL

BETWEEN the sudden sunlight and the rain
The birds sing gaily in the path wherethrough
I walk, and note the sky's ethereal blue,
Pure as the peace that's won, at last, from pain.
The sunshine and the sun-bright showers ordain
A festival of laughing flowers, whereto
The bees go buzzing past me; trees renew
Their lives of green: the whole land smiles again.

O April, longed for so through cheerless hours,
Thou who dost turn to silver winter's grey!
What is it ails thy skies, thy birds, thy flowers,
Gives to thy winds a mournful word to say,
And brings a sound of weeping with the showers—
What, but the thought of Aprils passed away?

MY GRAVE

FOR me no great metropolis of the dead—
Highways and byways, squares and crescents of death—
But after I have breathed my last sad breath,
Am comforted with quiet, I, who said—
'I weary of men's voices and their tread,
Of clamouring bells, and whirl of wheels that pass,'—
Lay me beneath some plot of country grass,

Where flowers may spring, and birds sing overhead:

Whereto one coming, some fair eve in spring,
Between the day-fall and the tender night,
Might pause awhile, his friend remembering,
And hear low words, breathed through the failing light,
In tone as soft as the wind's whispering,—
'Now he sleeps long, who had so long to fight.'

HER IN ALL THINGS

UNTO mine ear I set a faithful shell,
That as of old it might rehearse to me
The very music of the far-off sea,
And thrill my spirit with its fluctuant spell:
But not the sea's tones there grew audible,
But Love's voice, whispering low and tenderly,
Of things so dear that they must ever be
Unspoken, save what heart to heart may tell:

And hearing in the shell those tones divine—
Where once I heard the sea's low sounds confer—
I said unto myself, 'This life of thine
Holds nothing then which is not part of Her,
And all sweet things that to men minister
Come but from Love, who makes Her heart his shrine.'

OF EARLY VIOLETS

SOFT subtle scent, which is to me more sweet
Than perfumes that come later—when the rose
In all the splendour of her beauty blows—

Here, even to this busy London street,
Thou bringest visions of the grace we meet
When all-forgetful of the winters snows
The earth beneath the sun's kiss throbs and glows,
And answers to his strength with strong heart-beat.

Thou'rt like his lady's voice to one who waits,
In the dim twilight at her garden gates,
Her coming face—thou art the trembling rare
First note of Nature's prelude that leads on
The Spring, till the great, splendid orison
Of Summer's music vibrates in the air.

BELLS OF LONDON

As when an eager boy, I heard to-night
The selfsame bells clash out upon the air—
It seemed not then a city of despair,
But a fair home of promise and delight—
This London that now breaks me with its might.
Is this the end of all sweet dreams and fair?
Is this the bitter answer to my prayer?
The bells deride me from the belfry's height—

'We clamoured to thee in the old, far years,
And all the sorrows of thy life forecast;
And now, with eyes uncomforted by tears,
And dry and seared as by a furnace-blast,
Thou walkest vainly where no hope appears,
Between veiled future and disastrous past.'

A COUNTRY'S GHOST

SOME long dead Country's Ghost it surely is
Which haunts these Western waters—strange and bright
With dazzling gold of the sun's setting light,
Fair hills and fields it shows, but more than this
We may not know, since all its bane and bliss
Lie hidden in its cities, out of sight—
Strange cities, haply wrapt in sleep and night,
Where phantom lovers come again to kiss:

Or Ghosts of weary men by stealth come back
To climb the silent by-ways noiselessly—
Those ancient ways which no more dream of change,
Where still, I think, dead with their dead must range—
Ghost! seen a moment in the low sun's track,
Now hidden again in the concealing sea.

TO ALL SAD OF HEART

I HEARD one cry, 'The day is well nigh done;
The sun is setting, and the night is near—
The night wherein no moon or stars appear
And to whose gloom succeeds no joyful sun—
The race is ended, and the prize is won;
What prize hast thou?' I rose with heavy cheer,
Stretched empty hands, and said, 'No prize is here;
My feet were bruised, so that I might not run.'

Of victors wreathed I saw a goodly throng,
But turned mine eyes from these to where, apart,

Sad men moved wearily, with heads down-hung.
I cried, 'O ye who know Griefs poisonous smart,
Brothers! accept me, now ; for from my heart
To yours I send the passion of my song!'

TO ALL IN HAVEN

ALL ye who have gained the haven of safe days,
And rest at ease, your wanderings being done,
Except the last, inevitable one,
Be well content, I say, and hear men's praise;
Yet in the quiet of your sheltered bays,—
Bland waters shining in an equal sun—
Forget not that the awful storm-tides run
In far, unsheltered, and tempestuous ways:

Remember near what rocks, and through what shoals,
Worn, desperate mariners strain with all their might;
They may not come to your sweet restful ,goals,
Your waters placid in the level light;—
Their graves wait in that sea no moon controls,
That is in dreadful fellowship with Night.

FORECASTING

SOME day, as now, the world shall reawake:—
The city from its brief, dream-tortured sleep;
The country from its rest so pure and deep—
To songs of birds in every flowering brake;
And men light-hearted, or with hearts that ache,
Shall rise and go what they have sown to reap;
And women smile, or sit alone and weep

For life once sweet, grown bitter for love's sake:

But we, that day, shall not be here—not we—
We shall have done with life though few may know—
Between us then shall awful stillness be,
Who spake such words of bliss, such words of woe,
As winds remember, chanting fitfully—
Chanting, as now—above us lying low.

FRIENDSHIP AND LOVE

As feels the port for ships that come and go,
That tarry for a night, and in the day
Spread canvas and steer sailing far away
To other ports of which it may not know,
In unconjectured countries, even so
Man feels for man; nor long may friendship stay;
And little of its joy or its dismay
May any friend's heart to another show.

As feels the spirit of the melody
That, slumbering in a viol, a touch will start,
As feels the sun-thrilled sap within a tree,
So man and woman feel, when heart in heart
They live, and know this miracle to be,
In soul together, though to sense apart.

HERE IN THIS SUNSET SPLENDOUR DESOLATE

HERE in this sunset splendour desolate,
As in some Country strange and sad I stand—
A mighty sadness broods upon the land,

The gloom of some unalterable Fate.
O Thou whose love dost make august my state,
A little longer leave in mine thy hand—
Night birds are singing, but the place is banned
By stern gods whom no prayers propitiate.

Seeking for bliss supreme, we lost the track—
Shall we then part, and parted try to reach
A goal like that we two sought day and night,
Or shall we sit here, in the sun's low light,
And see, it may be through Death's twilight breach,
A new path to the old way leading back?

ALL ROUND ABOUT ME IS THE CITY'S NOISE

ALL round about me is the City's noise—
The pitiless clamour of the London street,
Wherethrough to-day I move with flagging feet:
Ah, shall I live, indeed, to hear thy voice;
Once more in thy dear beauty to rejoice,
To feel thy heart with mine give beat for beat—
Ah, Love, shall lips, and hands and spirits meet,
Dear Love, once more, before grim Death destroys?

Or shall Death come beforehand, in Love's place—
His semblance dark be set for dreadful sign?
O Love, if I no more should call thee mine,
Nor hold thee yet again in Love's embrace!
O Love, if thou no more shouldst own me thine,
Nor even thy tears be shed on my dead face!

O YE WHO SAILED WITH ME

O YE who sailed with me the evening seas,
Take to your boats now and depart, I say.
Ye know what winds and rains laid waste my day,
Yet how with even-song there came surcease;
But it is ended here my term of peace:
The sun has set—once more the sky turns grey,
And giant waves in menacing array
Surge on, and thunder, while the winds increase.

I must away, and sail to breast their might,
I—who once dallied by the fair sea side
Dreaming of stars, and gentleness of night—
Must go, now, with the inexorable tide,
Straight on to shipwreck, past each beacon light,
Till Death, his prey, from all men's sight shall hide.

BELOVED OF HER

THOSE people who are dear to her at all
Are for her sweet sake very dear to me—
All places known of her divinity
Are loved by me, and hold my heart in thrall:
These flowers, that felt her pure breast rise and fall,
Laid here apart where all her love-gifts be,
Are fragrant with the passionate memory
Of a dear day now lost past Love's recall:

Books she has read; least thing her hands have touched,
The very floor her garment's hem has brushed

Being loved of me, shall I not love as well
What she loved most—to climb the upward way;
No longer in this poppied vale to dwell,
But scale the heights where shines the perfect day?

COULD IT BUT BE!

COULD the sheer weight of suffering be laid
Upon my heart—if I for both might bear
The weariness, the horror, the despair,
The thoughts whereby the eyes become afraid
To close themselves in sleep; by grief dismayed
Watch the slow hours go by, while sobbing there
With broken wing comes back each outcast prayer
The soul in its wild agony has prayed:

If so I might take all the pain, and see
You walking happy with forgetful soul,
My image burned from out your memory,
Your dear feet hastening to some shining goal,
Then, surely, I could find grief ecstasy—
I could defy despair, your heart made whole.

NOT ONLY ROOMS WHEREIN THY LOVE HAS BEEN

NOT only rooms wherein thy Love has been
Hold still for thee the memory of her grace,
The benediction of her blessing face,
But other rooms that never saw thy Queen
Are full of her: Has not thy spirit seen
A vision of her in this firelit place

That never knew the witchery of her ways,
The perfect voice, the eyes intense, serene?

Ah, stood she not before the mirror there,
Her loveliness all clothed in soft attire,
Then turned to thee, low-kneeling by this fire,
And laid a gracious hand upon thy hair,
While thy heart leaped to her, thy heart's desire,
And thy kiss praised her, and thy look was prayer?

WHAT WAILING WIND

WHAT wailing wind of Memory is this
That blows across the Sea of Time to-day,
Blending the fragrance of a long-dead May
With breath of Autumn—agony with bliss?—
What phantom lips are these that cling and kiss,
And, kissing, clinging, find old words to say?
What parted days, in sad and glad array,
Rise up to haunt me from the grave's abyss?

Their tones subdue me, and their eyes confound,
So that I may not look from them to where
Each with its special message of despair,
In darkness habited, with darkness crowned,
Come on the days that rend, and will not spare,
Till in Death's sleep I, too, at last am bound.

I THOUGHT THAT I WAS HAPPY YESTERDAY

I THOUGHT that I was happy yesterday,
For though apart we stood soul close to soul,

So joined by infinite Love's supreme control
That happy spring danced with us on our way—
But now the brooding sky has turned to grey,
And heavily the clouds across it roll:
Oh, to what awful, unconjectured goal
Are our feet tending—my beloved one, say?

I dare not speak—dare hardly think of Love—
I am as one who not being dead yet hears
A sound of lamentation round his bed—
Feels falling on his face his friends' hot tears,
And, though he struggles inly, cannot move
Or say one word to prove he is not dead.

WHEN THOU ART FAR FROM ME

WHEN thou art far from me while days go by
In which I may not hear thy voice divine,
Or kiss thy lips, or take thy hand in mine,
walk as 'neath a dark and hostile sky,
And the Spring winds seem void of prophecy,
Nor is there any cheer in the sun's shine,
But present Grief and mocking Fear combine
To overthrow me when on Love I cry.

I am as one who through a foreign town
Journeys alone, some wild and wintry night,
And from the windows sees warm light stream down,
While there, for him, is neither heat nor light—
But far, far off, he has a lordlier home,
Whereto, one day, his weary feet shall come.

FOUR PARABLES

I
HEIGHT UPON HEIGHT

HEIGHT upon height, all washed by heavenly air
And crowned of heaven, I saw them rising free—
Those heights of Love, where I was fain to be—
And there I knew Love reigned, benign and fair;
With noble gifts for whoso enters there:
But, since between those heavenly heights and me
Stretched weary miles, with no compassionate tree
To shade me from the noon-tide's pitiless glare,
I paused brief while in a cool, wayside lane,
Under green boughs, and heard a strange bird sing,
But when I fain would struggle on again
Lo, round me Elfin things had drawn their ring,
And clouds shut out from me Love's shining height;
And Fate's strong sword flashed threatening in my sight.

II

ABOUT THIS LAND MOVES MANY A

SAD-EYED GHOST

ABOUT this land moves many a sad-eyed ghost,
And there is wail of weeping all night long,
And sounds by day of melancholy song:
Weird is the land, and beautiful, almost;
But wrecks of mighty ships strew thick the coast,

Though now the sea looks innocent of wrong,
And low, soft waves the deep sea-caverns throng,
Where sirens sing, and Death waits at his post.

Rise, rise, my soul, that we may strive with fate,
And flee the baneful beauty which delays
Us through warm, weeping nights and hectic days;
Spread sail and steer where fresh life may await:
But ah, what words sigh down these trackless ways—
What words but these: 'Too late—Too late—Too late'?

III

WALKED ONE SPRING DAY, WHILE

YET WINDS WERE COLD

I WALKED one spring day, while yet winds were cold,
Between the waning day and waxing night,
And the boughs strained and whirled in the wind's might.
I took a simple wild-flower in my hold,
And fair it was and delicate of mould,
And sweet to smell, and tremulous with light;
And something lurking in its petals white
Meant more to me than even its fragrance told.
Full long I held that flower, until one day
I came where queenliest, reddest roses grew;
Then from my hand afar that flower I threw,
Roses to gather; but, behold, this hour,
When roses and their thorn-stems strew the way,
I vainly seek for my lost woodland flower.

IV BEFORE THIS NEW LORD CAME

BEFORE this new Lord came into my house
It was a quiet place—within its halls
Were gracious pictures that made glad the walls
With hints of Southern slopes and olive boughs,
Or saints that wore bright halos on their brows—
But now that here the new Lord's footstep falls,
Now that his voice the ancient peace appals
Where once from dreams soft music did arouse:

Lo! all is changed. Gone the fair, pictured things,
And in their stead are many a grinning face,
And loathly shapes, and hurry of strange wings.
Shrieks rend the air, and blood-stained are the ways:
Yet—heard by me alone—a spirit sings,
This Lord shall not forever hold the place.

LOVE'S DESERTED PALACE

REGARD it well, 'tis yet a lordly place;
Palace of Love, once warmed with sacred fires,
Sounding from end to end with joy of lyres,
Fragrant with incense, with great lights ablaze.
The fires are dead now, dead the festal rays;
No more the music marries keen desires,
No more the incense of the shrine aspires,
And of Love's godhead there is now no trace.

Yet if one walked at night through those dim halls,
Might it not chance that ghostly shapes would rise,
And ghostly lights glide glimmering down the walls,
That there might be a stir, a sound of sighs,

And gentle voices answering gentle calls,
And wayward, wandering wraiths of melodies?

SPRING AND DESPAIR

THE cold spring twilight fills his lonely room—
There is no warmth, no fragrance on the air—
No song, but roll of traffic everywhere;
He dwells apart, in his own separate gloom,
Borne down by dread inevitable doom.
The bitter winds have left the young trees bare;
So wind-swept is his soul, no longer fair,
And withering slowly in a mortal tomb.

The early cold of spring shall pass away,
And June come on, of all sweet gifts possest,
With noons for rapture, and deep nights for rest;
But never any vivifying ray
Shall change for him one hour of any day
Till death's dark flower be laid on brow and breast.

LETHARGY

THIS is no midnight rent with thunder and fire,
Charged by mad winds, and wild bewildering rain;
Here is no great despair, no splendid pain,
But misty light, in which near things retire
And things far off loom close: No least desire
Is here: Why race?—There is no goal to gain;
Only one lethargy of heart and brain,
Which now not even Grief can re-inspire.

A sense of unseen Presences, that throng
The lonely room, the loud and populous street;
A sound from days long past, half wail, half song;
Death hurrying on, with swift, approaching feet;
Showing the man, as in a vision dread,
His cold, dead self stretched stiff upon a bed.

FROM LONDON STREETS

How fares it with my Love, in her far place?
I hear along the streets, this afternoon,
Thunder of wheels, and melancholy tune
Of church bells clashing over crowded ways.
To her of peerless heart and perfect face—
In whom is April wedded unto June—
Go now, my song, and breathe some mystic rune,
That she may think of far-off lovely days.

Oh, for my love's sake, and my soul's deep woe,
Be as a kiss upon dear lips and eyes—
Be warm about her, that her heart may know
The heart of one who is so little wise
That for the dreams and days of long ago
He seeks still with the spirit's diligent eyes

OUT OF SLEEP

FROM out dream-haunted coverts of dim sleep
A spirit staggers blindly toward the day,
Once more to face the old, unchanged dismay—
Once more to climb Life's desolate road and steep,
To sow his difficult field, and not to reap,

To look far up the dark and tedious way,
To see Death waiting at the end, to pray
That he may know prayer's worth, to watch and weep;

To linger in the once familiar place,
To talk with ghosts, frail ghosts that come and flee,
Some with kind eyes, some with reproachful gaze;
To see his unburied past stretched wretchedly
Across his path; and still forever face
Each pitiless day, till days no more shall be.

RESIGNATION

I thought in life to meet with Happiness,
And when, instead, Grief met me by the way
Most strange and bitter words I found to say;
But still I thought, through all the strain and stress
Of sorrowful living—through my life's excess
Of grief and loss—'Pain shall not always stay,
And fair may be the closing of my day;
Clear light and quiet may my evening bless!'

Then Happiness was shown me like the sun—
One flash and glory of triumphant light
Lit all my sky: but swiftly came the night
With waste winds wailing on the dead day's track;
And I am silent, now the day is done,
Knowing no words can bring its lost light back.

TO-MORROW

I SAID 'To-morrow!' one bleak, winter day—

'To-morrow I will live my life anew,'—
And still 'To-morrow!' while the winter grew
To spring, and yet I dallied by the way,
And sweet dear Sins still held me in their sway:
'To-morrow!' I said, while summer days wore through;
'To-morrow!' while chill autumn round me drew;
And so my soul remained the sweet Sins' prey.

So pass the years, and still, perpetually,
I cry, 'To-morrow will I flee each wile—
To-morrow, surely, shall my soul stand free,
Safe from the syren voices that beguile!'
But Death waits by me, with a mocking smile,
And whispers—'Yea! To-morrow, verily!'

SORROW'S GHOST

I SAW one sitting, habited in grey,
Beside a lonely stream ; and in her eyes
Was all the tenderness of twilight skies
In middle spring, when lawns are flushed with May.
'Mysterious one,' I cried, 'who art thou? Say!'
She answered in low tones, scarce heard through sighs:
'Look on this face! Dost thou not recognise
A face well known once, in another day?'

Then on the air these words grew audible:—
'The same she is who scorched thine eyes with tears;
But changed now by the sovereign force of years,
And piteous grown, and no more terrible:
Look on her now, who once thy life opprest—
Called bitterest Sorrow then; but now named Rest.'

LONDON, FROM FAR

AFAR from all this country peace it lies,
Tremendous and unscrutable for gloom—
The dreadful, fateful City of my doom.
I know its lurid, fog-invested skies—
I know what pestilential odours rise
From court and alley, each a living tomb—
I know the tainted flowers, by night that bloom
Along its wayside—flowers men spurn and prize.

I know the strife, and the unceasing din—
The utmost blackness of its heart I know—
I hear their shrieks and groans who toil within,
And cries of those it murdered long ago—
Yet mid the twisted growths of Shame and Sin,
One woodland flower of memory shall grow.

UNSHELTERED LOVE

LIKE a storm-driven and belated bird
That beats with aimless wings about his nest,
Straining against the storm his eager breast,
So is my love, which by no swift-winged word'
May enter at her heart, and there be heard
To sing as birds do, ere they fold in rest
Their wings, still quivering from the last sweet quest
When with their song and flight the air was stirred.

Oh, if some wind of bitter disbelief,
Some terrible darkness of estranging doubt,
Has kept it from thee, now, sweet Love, reach out
Thine hand and pluck it from this storm of grief:

It takes no heed of homeless nights and days.
So in thy heart it find its resting place.

WHEN IN THE DARKNESS I WAKE UP ALONE

WHEN in the darkness I wake up alone,
To face the loveless, desolated day,
What thought shall comfort, or what hope shall stay?
Ah Love, dear Love, Sweetheart that wast mine own,
Thou wilt not hear my spirit's bitter moan—
Thou wilt not see the terrible array
Of foemen marching on my destined way,
With ruthless hands and hearts more hard than stone.

I shall be left in those old ways to tread
Where Love and Sorrow walked with thee and me:—
For thee, ghosts of old days, unquiet dead—
Days glad in life, and sad in memory—
For me, to bow down weary heart and head
On dead Hope's grave, till I be dead as she.

A PRAYER TO SLEEP

O SLEEP, to-night be tender to my Love—
Hold her within thy clasp, so dear and deep—
Press gently on those sweetest eyes, kind Sleep:
Let no sad thought of me intrude, to move
Her heart to grief; but through some fair dream grove
Where faint songs steal, and gentle shadows creep,
And mystic stars and moons of dreamland keep
Their fond, persistent vigil, let her rove;

And if a dream of me must come, at all,
O show me to her glad with love and strong:
Let on her mouth my garnered kisses fall,
And to her ears make audible that song
I sang her once, when at her feet I lay,
At close of one divine, love-laden day!

I WALKED IN LOVE'S DESERTED ROOM

I WALKED in Love's deserted room alone,
And saw the lampless shrine, and in Love's place
Not Hope's transcendent light, nor met her gaze
Who, Queen of Love, made all my heart her own;
But a strange shape, as cold and hard as stone:
And round it pressed in that most desolate place
A phantom band, each one with ghastly face,
And each for some especial grief made moan.

I saw my Soul there, reigning in Love's stead,
And it cried out, 'Depart, ye clamouring throng—
While Joy or Grief was mine I gave ye song;
But now, behold my last song word is said:
Love is a frail thing; Death alone is strong,
And Hope, and Joy, and Grief with Love lie dead.'

TO THE SPIRIT OF POETRY

All things are changed save thee—thou art the same,
Only perchance more dear, as one friend grows
When other friends have turned away. Who knows
With what strange joy thou didst my life inflame
Before I took upon my lips the name

Which vows me to thy service? Come thou close;
For to thy feet, to-day, my being flows,
As when, a boy, for comforting I came.

Thou, whose transfiguring touch makes speech divine;
Whose eyes are deeper than deep seas or skies,
Warm with thy fire this heart, these lips of mine,
Lighten the darkness with thy luminous eyes,
Till all the quivering air about me shine,
And I have gained my spirit's Paradise!

OLD MEMORIES

WHAT olden memories are these that throng
To greet me on the threshold of this day—
Of buried hours what melancholy array?
Dull, now, the eyes that once were clear and strong—
Their lips but whisper that once thrilled with song—
Their grave-clothes are upon them, and they say—
'Know'st thou us still, and by what winding way
We led thy steps; nor did that path seem long?'

Yea, verily! I know ye but too well:
Your loving kindness once indeed was sweet—
Your deep joy subtler than a man may tell—
But why, with hearts that can no longer beat,
Why come ye back, and weave the olden spell
To daze my senses and perplex my feet?

GOOD-NIGHT AND GOOD-MORROW

THE fires are all burned out, the lamps are low,
The guests are gone, the cups are drained and dry.

A Last Harvest

Here there was somewhat once of revelry;
But now no more at all the fires shall glow,
Nor song be heard, nor laughter, nor wine flow.
Chill is the air; grey gleams the wintry sky:
Through lifeless boughs drear winds begin to sigh.
'Tis time, my heart, for us to rise and go
Up the steep stair, till that dark room we gain
Where sleep awaits us, brooding by that bed
On which who lies forgets all joy and pain,
Nor weeps in dreams for some sweet thing long fled.
'Tis cold and lonely now; set wide the door;
Good-morrow, my heart, and rest thee evermore.

www.bookjungle.com *email:* sales@bookjungle.com *fax:* 630-214-0564 *mail:* Book Jungle PO Box 2226 Champaign, IL 61825

The Codes Of Hammurabi And Moses
W. W. Davies

QTY

The discovery of the Hammurabi Code is one of the greatest achievements of archaeology, and is of paramount interest, not only to the student of the Bible, but also to all those interested in ancient history...

Religion **ISBN:** *1-59462-338-4* Pages:132 MSRP *$12.95*

The Theory of Moral Sentiments
Adam Smith

QTY

This work from 1749. contains original theories of conscience amd moral judgment and it is the foundation for systemof morals.

Philosophy **ISBN:** *1-59462-777-0* Pages:536 MSRP *$19.95*

Jessica's First Prayer
Hesba Stretton

QTY

In a screened and secluded corner of one of the many railway-bridges which span the streets of London there could be seen a few years ago, from five o'clock every morning until half past eight, a tidily set-out coffee-stall, consisting of a trestle and board, upon which stood two large tin cans, with a small fire of charcoal burning under each so as to keep the coffee boiling during the early hours of the morning when the work-people were thronging into the city on their way to their daily toil...

Childrens **ISBN:** *1-59462-373-2* Pages:84 MSRP *$9.95*

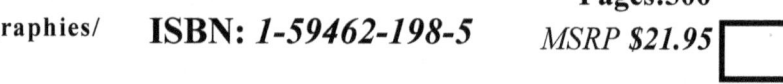

My Life and Work
Henry Ford

QTY

Henry Ford revolutionized the world with his implementation of mass production for the Model T automobile. Gain valuable business insight into his life and work with his own auto-biography... "We have only started on our development of our country we have not as yet, with all our talk of wonderful progress, done more than scratch the surface. The progress has been wonderful enough but..."

Biographies/ **ISBN:** *1-59462-198-5* Pages:300 MSRP *$21.95*

www.bookjungle.com *email: sales@bookjungle.com fax: 630-214-0564 mail: Book Jungle PO Box 2226 Champaign, IL 61825*

The Art of Cross-Examination
Francis Wellman

QTY

I presume it is the experience of every author, after his first book is published upon an important subject, to be almost overwhelmed with a wealth of ideas and illustrations which could readily have been included in his book, and which to his own mind, at least, seem to make a second edition inevitable. Such certainly was the case with me; and when the first edition had reached its sixth impression in five months, I rejoiced to learn that it seemed to my publishers that the book had met with a sufficiently favorable reception to justify a second and considerably enlarged edition. ..

Reference   ISBN: *1-59462-647-2*   Pages:412   *MSRP $19.95*

On the Duty of Civil Disobedience
Henry David Thoreau

QTY

Thoreau wrote his famous essay, On the Duty of Civil Disobedience, as a protest against an unjust but popular war and the immoral but popular institution of slave-owning. He did more than write—he declined to pay his taxes, and was hauled off to gaol in consequence. Who can say how much this refusal of his hastened the end of the war and of slavery?

Law   ISBN: *1-59462-747-9*   Pages:48   *MSRP $7.45*

Dream Psychology Psychoanalysis for Beginners
Sigmund Freud

QTY

Sigmund Freud, born Sigismund Schlomo Freud (May 6, 1856 - September 23, 1939), was a Jewish-Austrian neurologist and psychiatrist who co-founded the psychoanalytic school of psychology. Freud is best known for his theories of the unconscious mind, especially involving the mechanism of repression; his redefinition of sexual desire as mobile and directed towards a wide variety of objects; and his therapeutic techniques, especially his understanding of transference in the therapeutic relationship and the presumed value of dreams as sources of insight into unconscious desires.

Psychology   ISBN: *1-59462-905-6*   Pages:196   *MSRP $15.45*

The Miracle of Right Thought
Orison Swett Marden

QTY

Believe with all of your heart that you will do what you were made to do. When the mind has once formed the habit of holding cheerful, happy, prosperous pictures, it will not be easy to form the opposite habit. It does not matter how improbable or how far away this realization may see, or how dark the prospects may be, if we visualize them as best we can, as vividly as possible, hold tenaciously to them and vigorously struggle to attain them, they will gradually become actualized, realized in the life. But a desire, a longing without endeavor, a yearning abandoned or held indifferently will vanish without realization.

Self Help   ISBN: *1-59462-644-8*   Pages:360   *MSRP $25.45*

www.bookjungle.com *email: sales@bookjungle.com fax: 630-214-0564 mail: Book Jungle PO Box 2226 Champaign, IL 61825*

QTY

☐ **The Rosicrucian Cosmo-Conception Mystic Christianity** *by Max Heindel* ISBN: *1-59462-188-8* **$38.95**
The Rosicrucian Cosmo-conception is not dogmatic, neither does it appeal to any other authority than the reason of the student. It is: not controversial, but is: sent forth in the, hope that it may help to clear... New Age/Religion Pages 646

☐ **Abandonment To Divine Providence** *by Jean-Pierre de Caussade* ISBN: *1-59462-228-0* **$25.95**
"The Rev. Jean Pierre de Caussade was one of the most remarkable spiritual writers of the Society of Jesus in France in the 18th Century. His death took place at Toulouse in 1751. His works have gone through many editions and have been republished... Inspirational/Religion Pages 400

☐ **Mental Chemistry** *by Charles Haanel* ISBN: *1-59462-192-6* **$23.95**
Mental Chemistry allows the change of material conditions by combining and appropriately utilizing the power of the mind. Much like applied chemistry creates something new and unique out of careful combinations of chemicals the mastery of mental chemistry... New Age Pages 354

☐ **The Letters of Robert Browning and Elizabeth Barret Barrett 1845-1846 vol II** ISBN: *1-59462-193-4* **$35.95**
by Robert Browning and Elizabeth Barrett Biographies Pages 596

☐ **Gleanings In Genesis (volume I)** *by Arthur W. Pink* ISBN: *1-59462-130-6* **$27.45**
Appropriately has Genesis been termed "the seed plot of the Bible" for in it we have, in germ form, almost all of the great doctrines which are afterwards fully developed in the books of Scripture which follow... Religion/Inspirational Pages 420

☐ **The Master Key** *by L. W. de Laurence* ISBN: *1-59462-001-6* **$30.95**
In no branch of human knowledge has there been a more lively increase of the spirit of research during the past few years than in the study of Psychology, Concentration and Mental Discipline. The requests for authentic lessons in Thought Control, Mental Discipline and... New Age/Business Pages 422

☐ **The Lesser Key Of Solomon Goetia** *by L. W. de Laurence* ISBN: *1-59462-092-X* **$9.95**
This translation of the first book of the "Lernegton" which is now for the first time made accessible to students of Talismanic Magic was done, after careful collaition and edition, from numerous Ancient Manuscripts in Hebrew, Latin, and French... New Age/Occult Pages 92

☐ **Rubaiyat Of Omar Khayyam** *by Edward Fitzgerald* ISBN:*1-59462-332-5* **$13.95**
Edward Fitzgerald, whom the world has already learned, in spite of his own efforts to remain within the shadow of anonymity, to look upon as one of the rarest poets of the century, was born at Bredfield, in Suffolk, on the 31st of March, 1809. He was the third son of John Purcell... Music Pages 172

☐ **Ancient Law** *by Henry Maine* ISBN: *1-59462-128-4* **$29.95**
The chief object of the following pages is to indicate some of the earliest ideas of mankind, as they are reflected in Ancient Law, and to point out the relation of those ideas to modern thought. Religiom/History Pages 452

☐ **Far-Away Stories** *by William J. Locke* ISBN: *1-59462-129-2* **$19.45**
"Good wine needs no bush, but a collection of mixed vintages does. And this book is just such a collection. Some of the stories I do not want to remain buried for ever in the museum files of dead magazine-numbers an author's not unpardonable vanity..." Fiction Pages 272

☐ **Life of David Crockett** *by David Crockett* ISBN: *1-59462-250-7* **$27.45**
"Colonel David Crockett was one of the most remarkable men of the times in which he lived. Born in humble life, but gifted with a strong will, an indomitable courage, and unremitting perseverance... Biographies/New Age Pages 424

☐ **Lip-Reading** *by Edward Nitchie* ISBN: *1-59462-206-X* **$25.95**
Edward B. Nitchie, founder of the New York School for the Hard of Hearing, now the Nitchie School of Lip-Reading, Inc, wrote "LIP-READING Principles and Practice". The development and perfecting of this meritorious work on lip-reading was an undertaking... How-to Pages 400

☐ **A Handbook of Suggestive Therapeutics, Applied Hypnotism, Psychic Science** ISBN: *1-59462-214-0* **$24.95**
by Henry Munro Health/New Age/Health/Self-help Pages 376

☐ **A Doll's House: and Two Other Plays** *by Henrik Ibsen* ISBN: *1-59462-112-8* **$19.95**
Henrik Ibsen created this classic when in revolutionary 1848 Rome. Introducing some striking concepts in playwriting for the realist genre, this play has been studied the world over. Fiction/Classics/Plays 308

☐ **The Light of Asia** *by sir Edwin Arnold* ISBN: *1-59462-204-3* **$13.95**
In this poetic masterpiece, Edwin Arnold describes the life and teachings of Buddha. The man who was to become known as Buddha to the world was born as Prince Gautama of India but he rejected the worldly riches and abandoned the reigns of power when... Religion/History/Biographies Pages 170

☐ **The Complete Works of Guy de Maupassant** *by Guy de Maupassant* ISBN: *1-59462-157-8* **$16.95**
"For days and days, nights and nights, I had dreamed of that first kiss which was to consecrate our engagement, and I knew not on what spot I should put my lips..." Fiction/Classics Pages 240

☐ **The Art of Cross-Examination** *by Francis L. Wellman* ISBN: *1-59462-309-0* **$26.95**
Written by a renowned trial lawyer, Wellman imparts his experience and uses case studies to explain how to use psychology to extract desired information through questioning. How-to/Science/Reference Pages 408

☐ **Answered or Unanswered?** *by Louisa Vaughan* ISBN: *1-59462-248-5* **$10.95**
Miracles of Faith in China Religion Pages 112

☐ **The Edinburgh Lectures on Mental Science (1909)** *by Thomas* ISBN: *1-59462-008-3* **$11.95**
This book contains the substance of a course of lectures recently given by the writer in the Queen Street Hall, Edinburgh. Its purpose is to indicate the Natural Principles governing the relation between Mental Action and Material Conditions... New Age/Psychology Pages 148

☐ **Ayesha** *by H. Rider Haggard* ISBN: *1-59462-301-5* **$24.95**
Verily and indeed it is the unexpected that happens! Probably if there was one person upon the earth from whom the Editor of this, and of a certain previous history, did not expect to hear again... Classics Pages 380

☐ **Ayala's Angel** *by Anthony Trollope* ISBN: *1-59462-352-X* **$29.95**
The two girls were both pretty, but Lucy who was twenty-one who supposed to be simple and comparatively unattractive, whereas Ayala was credited, as her Bombwhat romantic name might show, with poetic charm and a taste for romance. Ayala when her father died was nineteen... Fiction Pages 484

☐ **The American Commonwealth** *by James Bryce* ISBN: *1-59462-286-8* **$34.45**
An interpretation of American democratic political theory. It examines political mechanics and society from the perspective of Scotsman James Bryce Politics Pages 572

☐ **Stories of the Pilgrims** *by Margaret P. Pumphrey* ISBN: *1-59462-116-4* **$17.95**
This book explores pilgrims religious oppression in England as well as their escape to Holland and eventual crossing to America on the Mayflower, and their early days in New England... History Pages 268

www.bookjungle.com email: sales@bookjungle.com fax: 630-214-0564 mail: Book Jungle PO Box 2226 Champaign, IL 61825

QTY

The Fasting Cure *by Sinclair Upton* ISBN: *1-59462-222-1* **$13.95**
In the Cosmopolitan Magazine for May, 1910, and in the Contemporary Review (London) for April, 1910, I published an article dealing with my experiences in fasting. I have written a great many magazine articles, but never one which attracted so much attention... New Age/Self Help/Health Pages 164

Hebrew Astrology *by Sepharial* ISBN: *1-59462-308-2* **$13.45**
In these days of advanced thinking it is a matter of common observation that we have left many of the old landmarks behind and that we are now pressing forward to greater heights and to a wider horizon than that which represented the mind-content of our progenitors... Astrology Pages 144

Thought Vibration or The Law of Attraction in the Thought World ISBN: *1-59462-127-6* **$12.95**
by William Walker Atkinson Psychology/Religion Pages 144

Optimism *by Helen Keller* ISBN: *1-59462-108-X* **$15.95**
Helen Keller was blind, deaf, and mute since 19 months old, yet famously learned how to overcome these handicaps, communicate with the world, and spread her lectures promoting optimism. An inspiring read for everyone... Biographies/Inspirational Pages 84

Sara Crewe *by Frances Burnett* ISBN: *1-59462-360-0* **$9.45**
In the first place, Miss Minchin lived in London. Her home was a large, dull, tall one, in a large, dull square, where all the houses were alike, and all the sparrows were alike, and where all the door-knockers made the same heavy sound... Childrens/Classic Pages 88

The Autobiography of Benjamin Franklin *by Benjamin Franklin* ISBN: *1-59462-135-7* **$24.95**
The Autobiography of Benjamin Franklin has probably been more extensively read than any other American historical work, and no other book of its kind has had such ups and downs of fortune. Franklin lived for many years in England, where he was agent... Biographies/History Pages 332

Name	
Email	
Telephone	
Address	
City, State ZIP	

☐ Credit Card   ☐ Check / Money Order

Credit Card Number	
Expiration Date	
Signature	

Please Mail to: Book Jungle
                    PO Box 2226
                    Champaign, IL 61825
or Fax to: 630-214-0564

ORDERING INFORMATION
web: *www.bookjungle.com*
email: *sales@bookjungle.com*
fax: *630-214-0564*
mail: *Book Jungle PO Box 2226 Champaign, IL 61825*
or PayPal *to sales@bookjungle.com*

Please contact us for bulk discounts

DIRECT-ORDER TERMS

20% Discount if You Order Two or More Books
Free Domestic Shipping!
Accepted: Master Card, Visa, Discover, American Express

www.ingramcontent.com/pod-product-compliance
Lightning Source LLC
Chambersburg PA
CBHW081327040426
42453CB00013B/2317